SOLOS FOR Kids

The student singers are from the Musical Theatre for Children workshop held at Southern Methodist University, Summer 1995, directed by Louise Lerch:

Amanda Addison, age 9
Puff the Magic Dragon

Sarah Hammond, age 11
How Much Is That Doggie in the Window
On Top of Spaghetti
The Rainbow Connection

Kaitlin Heller, age 12
Castle on a Cloud from *Les Misérables*

Bethy Thomas, age 13
Do-Re-Mi from *The Sound of Music*
Second Hand Rose
Take Me Out to the Ball Game

Joe Westergard, age 9
Hello Mudduh, Hello Fadduh! (A Letter from Camp)
I'd Do Anything from *Oliver!*
Little People from *Les Misérables*

This publication is not for sale in the E.C. and/or Australia or New Zealand.

ISBN 0-7935-4636-2

HAL•LEONARD
CORPORATION
7777 W. BLUEMOUND RD. P.O. BOX 13819 MILWAUKEE, WI 53213

D1275189

Copyright © 1995 by HAL LEONARD CORPORATION
International Copyright Secured   All Rights Reserved

For all works contained herein:
Unauthorized copying, arranging, adapting, recording or public performance is an infringement of copyright.
Infringers are liable under the law.

I'D DO ANYTHING
from the Columbia Pictures-Romulus film OLIVER!

Words and Music by
LIONEL BART

© Copyright 1960 (Renewed) Lakeview Music Co., Ltd., London, England
TRO - Hollis Music, Inc., New York, controls all publication rights for the U.S.A. and Canada
International Copyright Secured
All Rights Reserved Including Public Performance For Profit
Used by Permission

* When singing this song as a solo, this phrase in parentheses should probably be omitted.

Second Hand Rose

Words by GRANT CLARKE
Music by JAMES F. HANLEY

Copyright © 1921 Range Road Music Inc., Quartet Music Inc. and Sony Tunes Inc.
Copyright Renewed
All Rights on behalf of Sony Tunes Inc. Administered by Sony Music Publishing, 8 Music Square West, Nashville, TN 37203
International Copyright Secured   All Rights Reserved

THE RAINBOW CONNECTION

from THE MUPPET MOVIE

By PAUL WILLIAMS and KENNETH L. ASCHER

Why are there so man-y songs a - bout rain - bows, and
Who said that ev - 'ry wish would be heard and an - swered and when

what's on the oth - er side? _____
wished on the morn - ing star? _____

Rain - bows are vis - ions, _____ but on - ly il - lu - sions, And
Some - bod - y thought of that, and some - one be - lieved it;

Copyright © 1979 Jim Henson Productions, Inc.
All Rights Administered by Sony Music Publishing, 8 Music Square West, Nashville, TN 37203
International Copyright Secured   All Rights Reserved

CASTLE ON A CLOUD
from LES MISÉRABLES

Music by CLAUDE-MICHEL SCHÖNBERG
Lyrics by HERBERT KRETZMER
Original Text by ALAIN BOUBLIL and JEAN-MARC NATEL

Music and Lyrics Copyright © 1980 by Editions Musicales Alain Boublil
English Lyrics Copyright © 1986 by Alain Boublil Music Ltd. (ASCAP)
This edition Copyright © 1993 by Alain Boublil Music Ltd. (ASCAP)
Mechanical and Publication Rights for the USA Administered by Alain Boublil Music Ltd. (ASCAP)
c/o Stephen Tenenbaum & Co., Inc., 605 Third Ave., New York, NY 10158 Tel. (212) 922-0625, Fax (212) 922-0626
International Copyright Secured. All Rights Reserved. This music is copyright. Photocopying is illegal.
All Performance Rights Restricted.

LITTLE PEOPLE
from LES MISÉRABLES

Music by CLAUDE-MICHEL SCHÖNBERG
Original Text by ALAIN BOUBLIL and JEAN-MARC NATEL
Lyrics by HERBERT KRETZMER

Music and Lyrics Copyright © 1980 by Editions Musicales Alain Boublil
English Lyrics Copyright © 1986 by Alain Boublil Music Ltd. (ASCAP)
Mechanical and Publication Rights for the USA Administered by Alain Boublil Music Ltd. (ASCAP)
c/o Stephen Tenenbaum & Co., Inc., 605 Third Ave., New York, NY 10158 Tel. (212) 922-0625, Fax (212) 922-0626
International Copyright Secured. All Rights Reserved. This music is copyright. Photocopying is illegal.
All Performance Rights Restricted.

20

PUFF THE MAGIC DRAGON

Words by LEONARD LIPTON
Music by PETER YARROW

Copyright © 1963 by Honalee Melodies and Silver Dawn Music
Copyright Renewed
All Rights for Honalee Melodies Administered by Cherry Lane Music Publishing Company, Inc.
International Copyright Secured   All Rights Reserved

HELLO MUDDUH, HELLO FADDUH!
(A LETTER FROM CAMP)

Words by ALLAN SHERMAN
Music by LOU BUSCH

Hel-lo Mud-duh, hel-lo Fad-duh, here I am at Camp Gra-al-li-
na-da; Camp is ver-y en-ter-tain-ing, and they
say we'll have some fun if it stops rain-ing. I went hik-ing with Joe

coun-s'lors hate the wait-ers, and the lake has
ga-tors; And the head-coach wants no sis-sies, so he
reads to us from some-thing called U-lys-ses. Now I don't want this should

© Copyright 1963 by CURTAIN CALL PRODUCTIONS, INC.
Copyright Renewed
International Copyright Secured   All Rights Reserved

HOW MUCH IS THAT DOGGIE IN THE WINDOW

Words and Music by
BOB MERRILL

Copyright © 1952 Golden Bell Songs
Copyright Renewed 1980
Administered by All Nations Music
International Copyright Secured   All Rights Reserved

DO-RE-MI
from THE SOUND OF MUSIC

Lyrics by OSCAR HAMMERSTEIN II
Music by RICHARD RODGERS

Allegretto

Let's start at the ver-y be - gin - ing! ___

___ A ver-y good place to start, _____ When you

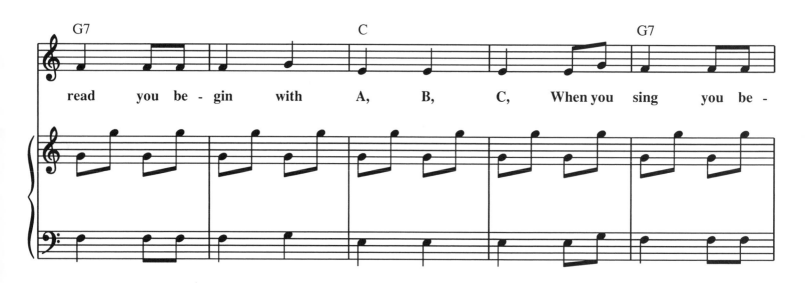

read you be-gin with A, B, C, When you sing you be-

Copyright © 1959 by Richard Rodgers and Oscar Hammerstein II
Copyright Renewed
WILLIAMSON MUSIC owner of publication and allied rights throughout the world
International Copyright Secured   All Rights Reserved

ON TOP OF SPAGHETTI

Words and Music by
TOM GLAZER

Copyright © 1963, 1965 by Songs Music Inc.
Copyright Renewed
Administered in the United States and Canada by September Music Corp.
International Copyright Secured All Rights Reserved

TAKE ME OUT TO THE BALL GAME

Words by JACK NORWORTH
Music by ALBERT VON TILZER

Copyright © 1987 by HAL LEONARD CORPORATION
International Copyright Secured   All Rights Reserved